A IS FOR ATHLETE

MICHAEL SAMPSON and BILL MARTIN JR

Illustrated by DAWN DAVIDSON

© 2024 Michael Sampson

All rights reserved. No part of this book may be used or reproduced in any manner without written permission except in the case of brief quotations embodied in critical articles or reviews.

A is for Athlete

Brown Books Kids
Dallas / New York
www.BrownBooksKids.com
(972) 381-0009

A New Era in Publishing®

Publisher's Cataloging-In-Publication Data

Names: Sampson, Michael R., author. | Martin, Bill, 1916-2004, author. | Davidson, Dawn, illustrator.
Title: A is for athlete / Michael Sampson and Bill Martin Jr ; illustrated by Dawn Davidson.
Description: Dallas ; New York : Brown Books Kids, [2024] | Interest age level: 004-008. | Summary: Team Bill Martin Jr and Michael Sampson step up to the plate in A is for Athlete to combine early literacy and world-renowned sports. Each letter is accompanied with facts that introduce the rules or provide history for each sport. From "A" is for Athlete to "Z" is for Zamboni and all letters in between, kids will not only grow more confident in their reading skills but might find a new sport or two that they want to learn.--Publisher.
Identifiers: ISBN: 978-1-61254-643-8 | LCCN: 2023948941
Subjects: LCSH: English language--Alphabet--Juvenile fiction. | Sports--Juvenile fiction. | CYAC: Alphabet--Fiction. | Sports--Fiction. | LCGFT: Alphabet books. | BISAC: JUVENILE FICTION / Sports & Recreation / General. | JUVENILE FICTION / Concepts / Alphabet.
Classification: LCC: PZ7.1.S2556 Ai 2024 | DDC: [E]--dc23

This book has been officially leveled by using the F&P Text Level Gradient™ Leveling System.

ISBN 978-1-61254-643-8
LCCN 2023948941

Printed in China
10 9 8 7 6 5 4 3 2 1

For more information or to contact the author, please go to
www.MichaelSampson.com.

MS–To Rhett Sampson and his love of sports

A IS FOR ATHLETE

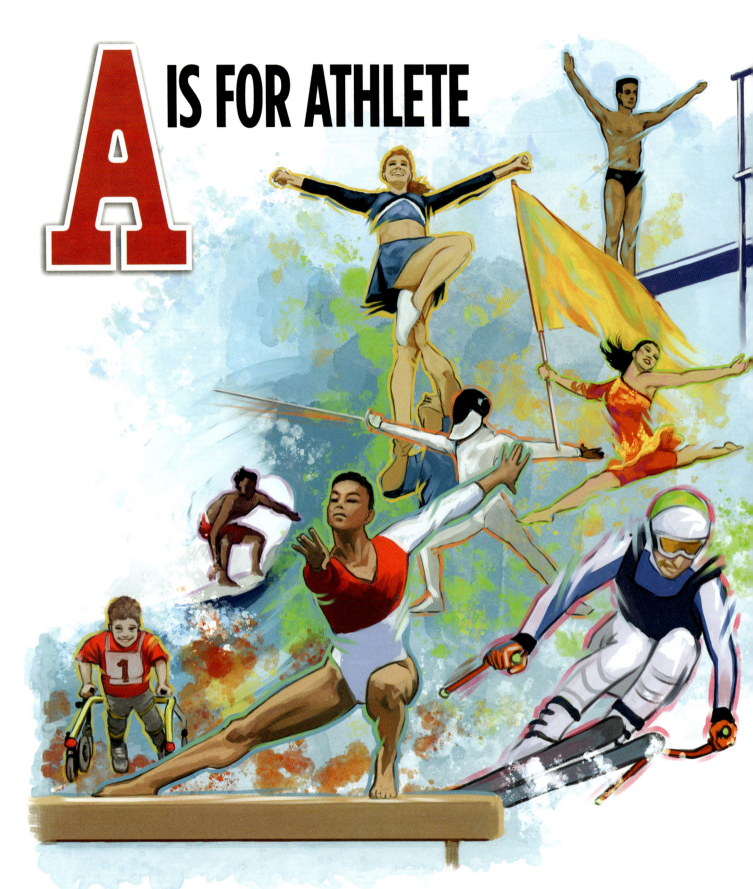

Athletes are the boys, girls, men, and women who play sports. They work hard and train their bodies to become the very best. Athletes are performers—they love the roar of the crowd as they score touchdowns in football or hit a twenty-foot jump shot in basketball.

B IS FOR BASEBALL

Often called "America's pastime," baseball became popular in the twentieth century when thousands of fans swarmed the ballparks to watch sluggers like Babe Ruth and Mickey Mantle hit home runs.

C IS FOR CURLING

Curling is like horseshoes but on ice. Players hurl a heavy stone with a handle on top across the ice toward a target, also called the house. An Olympic sport, curling is most popular in Scotland and Canada.

D IS FOR DRIBBLE

Basketball players bounce, or dribble, the ball with their hands as they run down the court. Some players can even dribble behind their backs! Dribble, dribble, **SWISH!**

E IS FOR EQUESTRIAN

The equestrian competition at the Olympics includes dressage, jumping, and eventing—a combination of dressage, cross-country, and show jumping. In the dressage competition, the horse and rider perform the same movements at different gaits to demonstrate control, pace, fluidity, and the rider's ability.

F IS FOR FOOTBALL

American football is played by little kids in Pop Warner leagues, in high schools, colleges, and in the NFL. The biggest game of the year is the Super Bowl, which is watched by 500 million people around the globe. Flag football will become an Olympic sport at the 2028 games in Los Angeles.

G IS FOR GOLF

Golf was invented in Scotland several hundred years ago. Today, millions of Americans play golf on beautiful courses throughout the United States. Thousands of fans attend Professional Golfers' Association tournaments and cheer for champion golfers like Scottie Scheffler.

H IS FOR HIGH JUMP

High jump is a track-and-field event in which athletes jump over a horizontal bar without knocking it down. The world-record for high jump is an amazing 1.45 meters!

I IS FOR ICE SKATING

Ice skating is essential in four different Winter Olympic sports: speed skating, figure skating, ice dancing, and hockey. Figure skating is the most popular of the three and includes a short program of mandatory jumps and skills and then a longer program, both set to music.

# J IS FOR JIU-JITSU

Jiu-jitsu, also called jujutsu, is a Japanese martial art that combines numerous fighting styles. The first school of jiu-jitsu was founded in the 1530s by Hisamori Takenouchi. It has inspired several modern martial arts and combat sports, including judo, aikido, and Brazilian jiu-jitsu. Jiu-jitsu gives you a deeper understanding of your body, mind, and spirit.

K IS FOR KARATE

Karate, an Olympic sport, is a martial art developed in Japan. Karate uses striking techniques such as punching, kicking, and knee and elbow strikes as well as using the side of your hand like a knife for a karate chop. Many youths around the world take karate classes. It takes about five years of training to become a black belt in karate.

L IS FOR LACROSSE

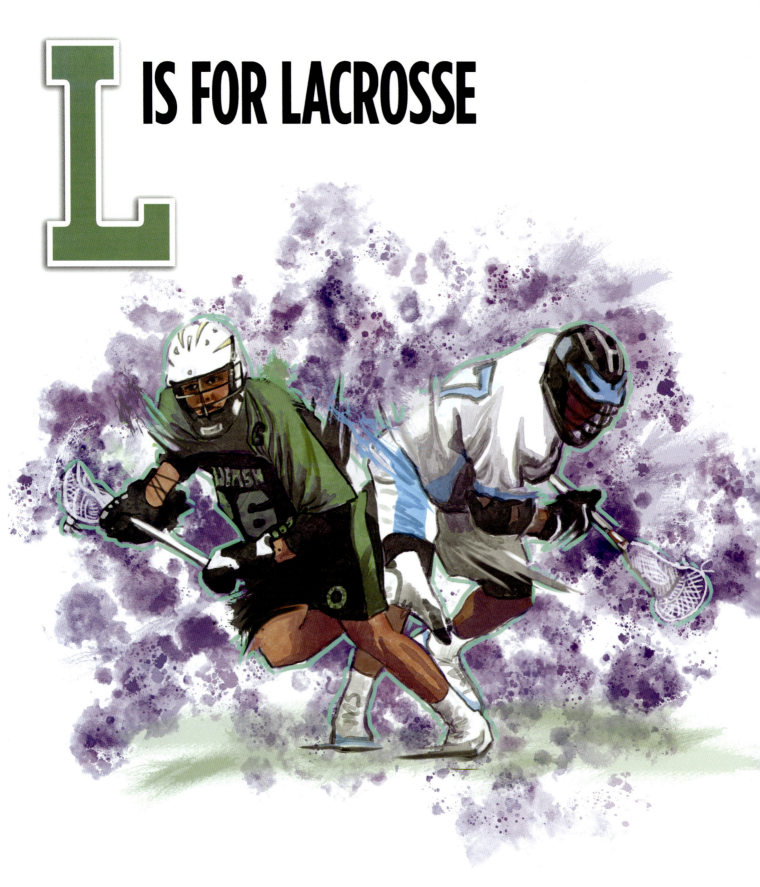

Lacrosse was first played by Native Americans and was called "baggataway." The French settlers adopted the game and named it lacrosse. This rough, physical-contact sport is played by teams of ten athletes who pass the ball toward the goal with a stick, or crosse, that has a mesh pocket.

M IS FOR MARATHON

A marathon is a 26.2-mile-long race that is run by hundreds of thousands of people in many different cities including Boston, New York, and Tokyo. Ever since the first race in Greece, athletes have run these races to achieve personal records and test their endurance.

 # IS FOR NASCAR

NASCAR (National Association for Stock Car Automobile Racing) is a popular spectator sport in America. Hundreds of thousands of race fans watch in amazement and cheer for their favorite driver as cars reach speeds of two-hundred miles per hour or higher and roar around the Winston Cup tracks.

O IS FOR OLYMPICS

These ancient Greek games were held at Olympia and included competitions in running, wrestling, and chariot racing. They reached great popularity in the eight to fourth century BC and continued until the end of the fourth century AD. The Olympics were resumed in Athens, Greece, in 1896. The Winter Olympics began in 1924 and included ice hockey, bobsledding, and skiing.

P IS FOR POLO

Water polo is a fascinating Olympic sport. It is played in a pool and has two teams of seven players who throw a ball toward their opponent's goal. Each team only has thirty seconds to score a goal before they have to give the other team control of the ball. The players wear colorful swim caps as they compete.

 # IS FOR QUIVER

A quiver is a round tube used to carry arrows in archery, which is the sport of using a bow to shoot arrows at a target. Quiver comes from the Anglo-French word *quivre*. A quiver usually holds about thirteen arrows. Robin Hood is a famous fictional character that uses a bow, arrow, and quiver.

R IS FOR RUGBY

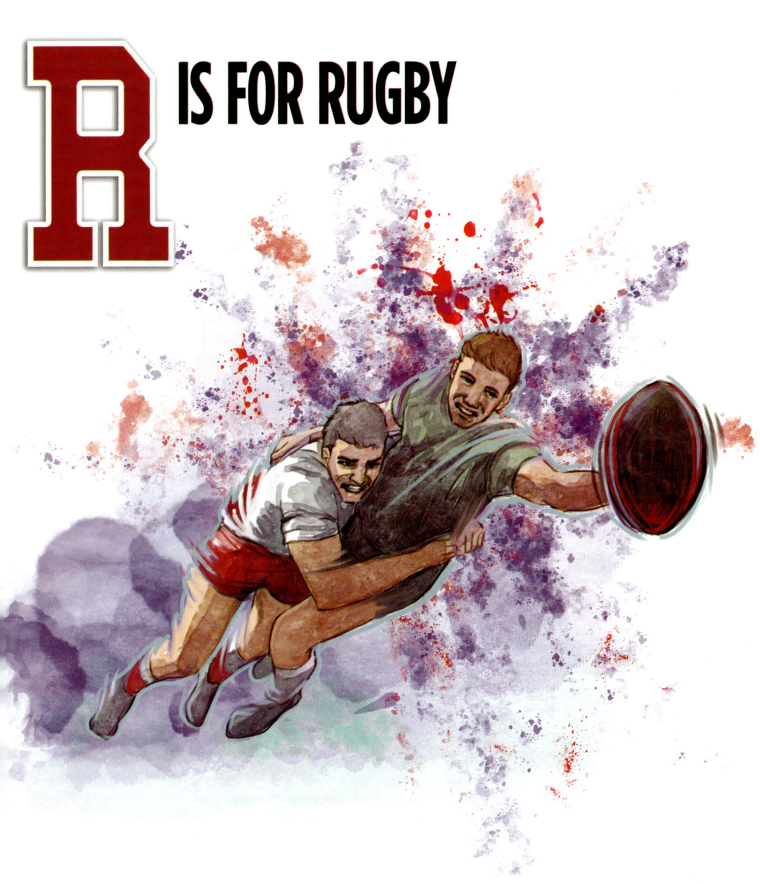

According to legend, the game of rugby started in Rugby, England, in 1823 when young soccer player William Webb Ellis picked up the ball and ran with it instead of kicking it. Rugby is similar to soccer and football and is very popular in Australia and England.

S IS FOR SOCCER

Organized soccer is one of the most popular sports in the United States. All you need is a ball, two goals, and players. Soccer is popular throughout the world and is often called "football."

T IS FOR TENNIS

Tennis has its origins in France and Great Britain. The game is played with one or two opposing players who trade volleys over a net in the center of the court. Tennis is played throughout the world, but the most prestigious tournament is still at Wimbledon, England, where the first Championship match was held.

U IS FOR UMPIRE

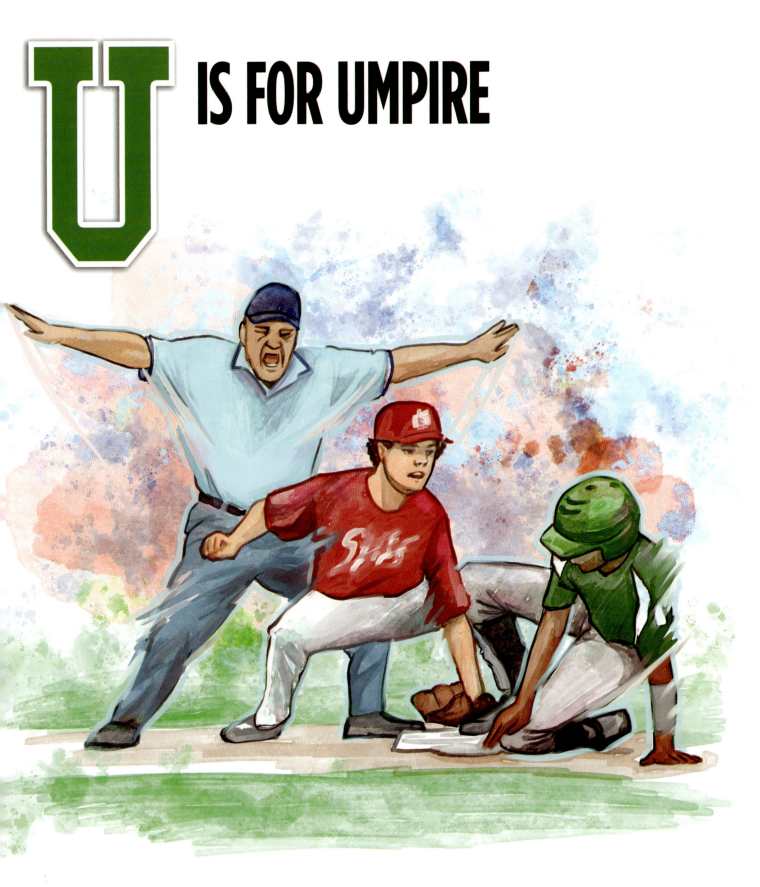

The umpire is the person in charge of the sport and makes sure that all the rules are followed. In some sports, they might be called a referee, like in soccer, or a judge, like in gymnastics. They make sure that all points are scored fairly. Although they are not always popular with fans, their presence is essential to fair competition.

 IS FOR VOLLEYBALL

Volleyball is played throughout America by high school, college, and professional players in organized leagues. However, volleyball is also an informal sport played at BBQs and on the beach. The object of the game is to knock the ball over the net to the other team in three or less hits without letting the ball touch the ground. Beach volleyball became an Olympic sport in 1996.

 # IS FOR WRESTLING

In ancient Greece, wrestlers were among the most popular Olympic heroes. Wrestling remains an Olympic sport, but its greater fame today comes from entertainment wrestling stars like Sami Zayn and Cody Rhodes. Past stars like the Rock and Triple H moved from wrestling to Hollywood fame.

X IS FOR THE X GAMES

The craziest sport of all is the X Games. Athletes from around the world compete for gold medals with dangerous maneuvers on skis and snowboards at the Winter X Games and on inline skates, skateboards, bicycles, and the climbing wall at the Summer X Games.

Y IS FOR YACHTING

The first yachts originated in the Netherlands where they were called *jaght* boats, or hunting boats. Today, athletes race their yachts in competitions like the America's Cup.

Z IS FOR ZAMBONI

When athletes "rough up" the ice, they need it smooth again. That's when a funny machine called a Zamboni is brought onto the ice. It whirls and swirls and makes the ice smooth. The machine was invented by Frank Zamboni more than fifty years ago.

The End